The Widow and the Bear

Tana Sommer-Belin

Cover photographs: Tana Sommer
Design: Kam Jacoby
Editing: Pauline Nelson
Copy editing: Kay Thompson Lee

SOMMER HOUSE BOOKS
162 Eucalyptus Hill Circle
Santa Barbara, California 93103 USA

Thanks to all the people who encouraged and helped in the writing of this book, and to Henri.

Lara woke up feeling nervous, as she did every morning. In the dim light, the time glowed red from her alarm clock: 5:45. The day loomed ahead and Lara hugged Henri, her stuffed teddy, a little harder. The hug worked well against loneliness. Soon she would feel able to sit up and think about the day, and Henri often helped with that as well. She would discuss her plans with him, poking his tummy now and then, and Henri would generally agree with whatever she said. He was a flexible guy.

Sometimes Lara wondered if it was a bad sign that, at fifty-seven, she was sleeping with and confiding in a toy bear. What would Pierre say, if he were here? But of course, if he were here, filling his side of the bed as he had done for twenty-three years, she would not need Henri. Twenty-three years, and the only time apart was the one summer she did not go to France with Pierre and their daughter Julie.

Lara figured it out once on a calculator: 8,350 nights they had slept together.

It was Julie who bought her the bear after Pierre's death a few months ago. She was away at college now, but she understood how things were. She knew it was tough for Mom to sleep alone, and she knew Mom loved bears. Lara used to call Pierre "bear" sometimes, although she used the French word—"*Ours*"—because he was French. Her French bear: a strong, big man, six-and-a-half feet tall, who gave a great hug and loved honey on his morning toast, or better yet, straight out of the jar on a spoon.

Lara gazed across the king-size emptiness of the bed. She and Henri rumpled hardly one third of it. She looked around the room, with its fine north facing window and thought, as she sometimes did, that she should turn it into a studio. She could take the bed out and sleep on a couch. It was just a bed: one of a long list of things that had once been a part of married life but that now seemed useless.

But she couldn't give it up, not yet. It was almost as if Pierre might come back; she would wake up from this nightmare and he would be back in the kitchen cooking *Boeuf Bourguignon*, the wonderful smell permeating the whole house, and everything would make sense again.

Instead, she awoke feeling anxious every day. Even after a long hug with Henri.

At least the sun was shining; the shades were brightening now, and she could hear the birds. When it was dull and foggy and the light was gray, it was so hard to get up. On those days, Dr. Bridges had told her: "You've got to hit the ground with your feet, straight out of bed and get going. The big mistake is to look out from under the covers at the dimness and say 'why?'" Then the whole existential dilemma of the meaning of life would start to unroll in a huge tangled mess, and she'd never even get dressed.

Yes, *hit the ground*. Even if she had to pretend there was some reason to do it. It was easier if she had no choice: maybe someone was coming—the housecleaner, or the piano teacher—or maybe her mother had a doctor's appointment to be taken to.

This morning the promise of sunlight was enough. She lifted the shades at the window and looked out to see the sun catch the dusty purple spikes of lavender. *Stay in the moment*, she thought. As long as she hung onto the present moment, and the present moment looked good, she was okay.

Now: breakfast. "Ready for breakfast, Henri?" She picked the bear up off the bed and tweaked his big, round nose. Of course Henri didn't need to be asked. If honey was on the menu, he was always ready.

On her way to the kitchen Lara turned on the computer, anticipating an email from her friend, Christine, in France, who'd lost her husband two years earlier. Christine had three grown sons but wanted to appear strong for them, which had left her no one else to cry with but Lara. Email was not ideal, but it was better than nothing, and Lara wrote to Christine every day, giving her someone to talk to and complain to, cutting into her new loneliness.

Those daily emails were filled with the shared joys of their creative interests—they talked of writing projects and stories, of houses, gardens, animals and kids.

And, of course, grief. For two years Christine had poured out her pain, and Lara had listened. Now, just as Christine was beginning to feel like her old self again, it was Lara who needed a friend to listen, and Christine was there. Even from six thousand miles away, her emails comforted Lara, but she wondered now, as the kettle boiled for tea: would it take *her* two years to feel like herself again? Would the road really be that long?

After breakfast Lara sat down at the computer with her cup of tea, eager to communicate with Christine about the things that really counted. In other seasons of her life she would have spent this morning time doing yoga, knee exercises, Tai Ji or meditation. All were good ways to start the day but they included no dialogue. Oh, yes, there was internal dialogue, but Lara was sick of that. Round and round in her head, the voices—so judgmental, so reprimanding, even of her knees, her stiff muscles—made it all another trial.

It was so different when Pierre was there. His devotion had renewed her each day. If he could love her that much, she must be worthwhile. Without him, she had her doubts. She had a stack of self-help books on her nightstand big enough to threaten an avalanche, but they could not give her that belief in herself, a self worth exploring, worth expressing. Now she wondered: had her sense of being loved disappeared with her husband?

The Hospice counselor told Lara that she did not have to lose Pierre; he was still there for her with all he did and said all those years. All Lara knew was that she now slept with a teddy bear, and that warm visceral support was gone. She'd have to float her own boat—become self-reliant—and some days that seemed impossible.

*

Lara's attention was pulled away from the computer by a scratching sound at the door. She looked up to see the face of Lucie the dog, waiting to come in from her sleeping spot on the porch. She got up and let the Airedale in, welcoming the joyful, loving energy she brought with her.

Lucie missed Pierre too, especially in the first weeks he was gone, but she had a dog's Zen wisdom and lived thoroughly in the NOW. On a sunny day she could be counted on for a romp and a game of ball; if it drizzled all day she'd use her time wisely and sleep. Lara often envied Lucie the simplicity of her life. Could she somehow replicate it? It felt as if a partial lobotomy would be needed, just to cut out the nagging doubts and useless thoughts of the past that plagued her.

Lara couldn't even keep her New Year's resolution to take more walks with Lucie and observe the wise four-footed one. Time management: maybe that was the issue. Where did her time go? There never was enough of it. She envied people who only slept six hours a night. Maybe if she went to bed later she could have a beautiful pristine desk too, every paper filed or tended to.

"Come on," she said now, scratching Lucie's furry head. "Let's go get the newspaper." It wouldn't exactly be a workout for Lucie, but it would get Lara outside, where she could greet the day. *Breathe in the immensity of nature*—it was part of her Tai Ji practice, and, while it didn't cut out her nagging thoughts as swiftly as a lobotomy might, she was grateful for the touchstone it provided.

The garden was damp and shady, and Lucie darted here and there as Lara walked to the end of the drive and picked up the newspaper. She pulled it out of its plastic wrap, glanced at the headlines, and felt her spirits dip. War, politics, doom and gloom.

Walking back to the house, watching Lucie frisk here and there, Lara thought back to her first moments on waking: always nervous, anxious. It was worse without Pierre, but she had to admit that no matter what her life circumstances had been, she always woke up worried. Except on vacation. Her psyche somehow felt free to take a break then and just wake up, like Lucie did, with no questions asked. She stepped back into the kitchen; Henri was still sitting on the counter.

"I need to be on permanent vacation," she told him, "always traveling, living out of a suitcase, unavailable!" She tossed the newspaper aside. "That's what we'll do when I win the lottery." Henri felt that he did not have anything to contribute to that conversation, as he had not traveled much, did not pay attention to the news, and would only be interested in a honey lottery.

But would it make any difference to escape, to wander the world? wondered Lara. Her friend the therapist had helped her to see that she was looking for externals to change, and had given up on her internal landscape. Antidepressants helped her avoid the dark black pit of immobilization, but they did not help much with the *raison d'être*. Lara did not see herself taking up a religion at this late date, nor did she want to end up at a bar, drowning out all sensation, the good with the bad.

There had to be a way to venture forward into the next phase of her life. She should follow Lucie's example, spend time among the blooming roses. Whatever she did, she needed to find the brush to bring color back to her blank canvas.

That night, as she got ready for bed, Lara looked around for Henri and found him sitting next to one of her favorite pictures of Pierre. He seemed to be studying the wise and smiling face, the easy, elegant demeanor, the glass of wine lifted in a toast. "I wish you could have met him," said Lara, lifting Henri down from the shelf and hugging him hard. "You sometimes remind me of him." It was true: both of them were able to be entirely present in the moment and had no time for worries, and both of them had a way of communicating their calm to her when she needed it. Henri assumed that she was referring to another, obvious similarity: that Pierre was a fellow honey lover, and, therefore, an evolved man in touch with the good life.

*

The morning light was gray a few days later. Lara awoke feeling tired and achy, with the beginnings of a sore throat. This was the kind of day when she longed to pull the covers up and stay in bed, but the carpenter was coming to start the new fence at 8 a.m., and Henri gave her a stern look.

"I know: *feet on the ground*," she groaned, pushing back the covers and easing her feet to the floor. On her way to the kitchen she switched on the computer, but there was no message from Christine this morning. She walked down the driveway in the early chill with Lucie to get the paper. More bombs in Baghdad; now she felt even worse. Back in the kitchen, she dropped the paper into the recycling bin and looked at Henri with a sigh. "Maybe I should cancel poetry writing with Sandra."

Henri pondered this for a moment. He did not really see the point of writing poems, but he knew it was good for Lara to get out and see a friend. And if covering lots of paper with lots of squiggles took some of those round-and-round thoughts out of Lara's poor head, then that was good, too. He was glad he was a bear and did not have to resort to such measures; a well-timed nap solved most of his problems.

In the end, Henri pointed out that Lara should not make any decision about the day on an empty stomach, and that the first thing she needed was a cup of hot tea. Lara put on the kettle, and by the time the carpenter arrived she was feeling better and looking forward to seeing Sandra.

After discussing the plans for the new fence, she drove up to Santa Ynez, her heart lifting at the sight of the golds and greens of the valley. The journey passed swiftly, and soon she was greeting her friend with a kiss on each cheek. Sandra had been through a lot in life, but she still had her husband, and Lara envied her that. Sandra joked about how predictable he was; she had even written a poem about how he always wanted to go to the same restaurant and order the same thing. But Lara saw a handsome, energetic man who was totally in love with his wife, and that seemed like a lot to her.

Today, though, Sandra was wrestling with fresh grief of her own: her best friend had died just a week earlier, of lung cancer. Death was around them again: this time claiming a mother of nine (four of hers, four of his, one of theirs) who used to bake four loaves of bread a day. Lara thought anyone so full of life and courage should not die at seventy.

But Death had its own schedule, and all Sandra and Lara could do was write about their losses. They wrote for hours: ten-minute poems that started and ended with the *brrinngg* of a kitchen timer. Every subject was thrown about, taking off from words found in the newspaper: "bait," "squander," "water," "berserk." Sandra's poems tended toward mini-stories, complete with dialogue, all in fifteen lines. Some touched on memories from way back. She took the word "squander" and rewound a reel of her life to the day when she spent her first allowance on comic books and a Baby Ruth bar. When she got home her Dad said, in his thick Mississippi accent, "Sandra K, you have squandered all your money, and now you have nothin' left to give Jesus on Sunday!"

Sandra's poems always contained people; Lara's poems were more vague and philosophical. Was this the style of an only child who grew up without the running dialogue of a large family in her ears? For Sandra, the past was vividly present, with all its color and sound. Lara rarely used to think about the past, being more concerned with what the future had in store. Now, though, she thought daily about Pierre, and what it had been like to live with such a warm, generous, smart man.

Today's poems touched on love, death, pranks, murderers, animals and barbed wire. The two poets' minds spread out on paper like a wild smorgasbord of images. As always, they read the words out loud to each other, but by mid-afternoon Lara's voice began to scratch, and she could hardly read the last poem.

By the time she got home she felt bad enough that she considered skipping her evening yoga class. She looked at Henri, once again leaning up against a photo of Pierre, as if he were getting to know him. One thing that had always struck her about Pierre was that he seemed comfortable in his body. He never acted like an invalid, even though he had already had a heart attack when she first met him, and he knew for the last year of his life that he could die at any time.

Act the way you want to feel. One of those books on her nightstand said something like that. All right then, she would *pretend* she was healthy. She would go to yoga.

It was a struggle. Her muscles ached and resisted, but posing outside on the grass facing the ocean towards sunset was a treat, and in that instant Lara felt present in the moment, and grateful. The complete opposite, in fact, of how she had felt upon awakening that very morning. The doctor was right: you have to hit the ground and get going. Who knows what can happen later in the day?

That night Henri tucked himself in close beside Lara and reminded her that she should stock up on honey soon. "We don't want to lose track of the essentials," he murmured before drifting off to sleep. He really had an astonishing vocabulary for a bear his size.

*

The next morning, Lara still felt the sore throat and lagging energy of the day before. She got up sniffling, and headed for the bottle of Echinacea. *Probably too late, but let's try some more of this stuff,* she thought. *And **positive thoughts**: this infection (whatever it is) is going to pass right by, real fast. I am basically* *healthy. I see myself as healthy.* She recited all the health-giving mantras she could remember, quoting everyone from Adele Davis to Deepak Chopra. Henri scoffed at all this, saying a good dose of morning honey would sort out all her problems. Lara poked him in the tummy. "If I ate honey every time you told me to, I'd have a different problem. I'd be as round as you are." Henri chose not to reply.

It was foggy again, and when Lara came in from outside with the newspaper, Henri could smell the damp sweetness of the garden. But Lara did not look as though she had smelled any sweetness; she was reading the front page headlines and looking upset. Henri was young and inexperienced, but he knew that it was his job to help Lara feel better. Julie had told him so in the toy store, when she had chosen him. So he cleared his throat and made a suggestion: maybe Lara should stop getting the newspaper.

At first he was not sure she had heard him, but after a minute she sighed and said, "You're probably right, but...oh, boy...another transition to think about. We've been getting the local paper for fifteen years. Pierre read it every day. He was news-hungry." She smiled at the memory, then her face clouded again. "It feels...sacrilegious to cancel."

Henri pointed out that, on the other hand, she would be saving trees and not feeling so gloomy every morning. She needed to think about her blood pressure! She could be reading Baudelaire instead of bad news with her morning toast!

Lara was secretly impressed by all of Henri's suggestions, but she had one last objection: "I don't want to be an ostrich with my head in the sand. I need to stay in touch with what's happening in the world."

Then, before Henri could say it himself, she added, "Of course, NPR gives me all the news I really need. And...Baudelaire with my morning toast? Why, Henri, I didn't think you cared about poetry!" Lara picked up the fat little bear and squeezed him tight, congratulating him for his wise reasoning.

"Oh, *mon petit ours*, making a decision feels good!"

Henri agreed, but said that he was now exhausted and ready for the first nap of the day, which he would take on the couch. He suggested that Lara go out and do something that she liked.

So she did. She went to buy compost.

Gardening and planting always made Lara feel good. It made her feel as if there would be a future, even if she, as a new widow, could not visualize the upcoming bouquets. At the nursery she fell in love with a huge grapevine throwing off tendrils in all directions. Her spirits rose, calling up images of her dream of being *une châtelaine* in France: she would be the landowner of a large property, her house set in the middle of a vineyard, so that every day could begin with a look out of an upstairs window over the vines below. Lara had entertained this fantasy for at least twenty-five years.

Yes, this tall, magnificent grape would find a home in Santa Barbara and live alone by the new fence, hiding the trash cans. Some lavender plants would complete the scene, a miniature gesture towards a large dream. Lara had missed France all the more since Pierre died. He was her true French connection. Even in California they could pretend they were in France—speaking French all the time, cooking French meals, drinking French wines, hosting French guests, and telephoning the French family—all in the soft Santa Barbara climate that was particularly good for Pierre's health. In his absence Lara made a point of finding places to speak French: a dinner conversation at Chez Patrice, a friend's conversation group, and a French-speaking women's lunch group were all regular fixtures on the calendar.

Transforming the rear entrance to the house felt like raising the French flag: small steps toward a far-off dream. Lara worked all afternoon, enjoying the smell of the soil and the sight of the vigorous young plants. She stood back and surveyed the effect. It was good. It was enough for today.

And it would have to be enough for a long while, because the failing health of Lara's elderly parents' put any hope of a long sojourn in France on indefinite hold. They were in their nineties, still living in their home, and, as their only child, Lara felt the full responsibility of their care. Doctors' appointments, bills, insurance, taxes, repairs, linens, shopping...with so much to manage, she could not possibly leave the country except for a short break, and even then only if she organized a battery of support systems.

All these transitions! Once a wife, now single; once a child, now a parent to her parents; once a mother to her young child, now seeing that child grown and making her own transitions, moving for the first time into a place of her own. Meanwhile, what had become of the independent artist Lara had once been? It felt as if she'd been gone for years. Was she still around somewhere?

Lara put away her gardening tools and gloves and went inside. She was glad to have accomplished so much today, to have made decisions on her own. But she felt overwhelmed so often, and yearned for a clear strategy to get her through this tumultuous period.

Creating a strategy, though, was not a simple task. Lara felt like she was walking on Jell-O all the time. No firm ground to push against when taking the next step. Everything moved when she moved; it was dizzying. The Hospice grief counselor had said, "Expect to feel strange and disoriented for a long time." She was not kidding.

Oh well, Lara thought, *it's not like I'm really a free agent...I'm parenting my parents, so that's my raison d'être. Maybe I should focus on that, and let a single French grapevine symbolize the rest of my personal dreams.* It was not a very happy prospect.

Henri agreed with Lara that it was hard to muster enthusiasm for the future; that's why he thought it was a much better idea to live one day at a time, one hour at a time. He reminded her to breathe, eat good food, sit in the garden, speak French with her funny-sounding friends, and play the piano, even if she didn't play brilliantly. "I can stand it!" he promised. (It was true; Henri was very tolerant of her ragged practicing, unlike Julie, who, if she were home, would sigh and close all the doors between them.)

One night Lara found the book *The Power of Now* on her pillow, and guessed that Henri had put it there. "I've already read this," she said.

Henri gave her a pointed look and said he thought it was time for her to read it again. She climbed into bed and pulled him into a cuddle. She felt herself relax into sleep as Henri murmured into her ear all the important things she needed to remember: your *now* has nothing to do with what happened yesterday, or what is going to happen tomorrow or the next day... you see a lot of closed doors right now, and no open windows yet, but one day— surprise!—there *will* be a window and you will look out and see something new...and in the meantime, follow my strategy: stock up the larder with honey so that there's at least one thing every day to be happy about, and focus on the small, reliable things, like I do...

*

One morning, about six months after Pierre died, Lara woke to sunshine so brilliant it pierced through the pinholes in the window blinds, like stars on a night sky. The last three days had been hot, unusual for the central coast of California. Although it was only early May, the whole garden was bursting into flower and thirsting for water.

Henri was already sitting up against the pillows, bright-eyed and thinking about breakfast. Lara looked at the patterns the sunlight cast onto the walls and said, "Henri, with any luck, today, I am finally going to paint. Yes, *really* paint, and in oil, for the first time since Pierre died."

Getting up was a lot easier that day. Lara opened the blind and the sunshine poured in; her bare feet felt warm on the wood floors.

Lucie was waiting to greet her at the porch door. It was time to think of a new morning routine for them to share, now that there was no newspaper to fetch. Preferably the routine should still include walking the length of the driveway where numerous balls and toys lay ready to throw. An idea came to mind. They could pretend they were Zen monks, and go around and greet all the flowers, trees and ivy, and see how everything looked in the early morning light.

So they did. Visiting the flowers was nothing new for Lucie, but as long as she still got the occasional biscuit, she was happy to tag along while Lara talked to the plants. For Lara, the new routine was a great improvement. *One can choose the manner in which one wants to start the day*, she thought, pausing to smell a fragrant pink rose. Another idea struck her: from now on she could keep the clippers on the front porch, and go back into the house with a fresh bouquet. *I am making changes*, she thought.

Henri had skipped the flower-greeting ritual since Lucie

was there to look after Lara. He was waiting in the kitchen when She came in, carrying flowers. She began to hum as she arranged them, and Henri thought about those other mornings when Lara would come in carrying the newspaper, and begin to rant about the futility of war. Humming was much nicer, in his opinion.

They had breakfast, with Henri literally sticking to the only item on the menu he cared for. Why bother with toast? It only made you fatter. Lara smiled, remembering Pierre's similar fondness for a spoonful of honey straight out of the pot. She had her usual half grapefruit, buttered toast and strong black tea.

Lara needed to read something with her tea as Pierre was not there and Henri was too busy eating to chat. She decided to read the French weekly paper *Le Monde Hebdomedaire*. Printed on thin paper and only a few pages long, it was destined for French people on foreign soil and gave a more international perspective on the world's news. More importantly, it had no upsetting photos.

Today there was a long article about a small African country she did not even know existed. Discovering how little she knew about the world in general was a pet peeve of hers. "By my age I should know things like this!" she told Henri. "Instead it feels like the older I get the less I know."

Henri did not comment, partly because it was difficult to talk with his mouth full, but also because he was a young bear who did not trouble himself too much with knowing the names of things.

"Getting older is turning out to be the most humbling experience of my life," Lara concluded, "apart from motherhood."

Henri did not like the turn the conversation had taken, so he was happy to see Lara get up and go out into the sunshine to perform a round of her Tai Ji Five Elements. She would feel better after that, he was sure.

And when she came in from the brightness of the garden, Lara did feel better. It was time to paint.

She got out her tubes of oil paint and squeezed some amber, purple, and green onto her palette. The distinctive smell of the oils filled the room, and she relished—as she always had—the buttery texture of the paint under her brush. And yet she found it hard to begin. Doubtful, fearful thoughts skittered through her mind: *Can I still do this?*

Then, as if he were standing right next to her, Lara heard Pierre's voice, encouraging and enthusiastic. *"Allez, allez!"* he said, hushing her doubts. *"Allez*—go on, do it!" Lara closed her eyes and breathed, steadying herself.

Now, she wondered, **what should I paint?** She remembered the so-called homework assignment the Hospice counselor had given her. "Paint me a painting of your feelings," Mary had said. "Not a landscape, not a still life, no people, just your feelings. It does not matter how it looks." Lara did not usually paint that way. Normally the subject drew her in and made her want to paint it: a lavender field, red poppies, the sea. Her feelings were never the subject themselves, but they found their way somehow into the brush strokes, the light.

But that was before. Now, when every part of her life seemed to be in transition, *why not just go ahead?* Lara thought. *Allez! Get the brushes wet again and try not to think too much. Just go directly from the heart, to the paint-filled brush, to the canvas.*

Yellow came first, a big swirl in the middle of the canvas— a glow, surrounded by a magenta pink swirl, then more yellows and gold and whites, whirling out to the edge. Then, about twenty minutes later, a deep indigo rolled across the bottom of the canvas.

Bach played in the background, Lucie lay in a slant of sunlight on the floor, and Henri napped in the wingback chair, dreaming of his next meal. For the first time in six months, all seemed right with the world. Even Pierre was there in Lara's head, chasing the doubts away and urging her on, encouraging her to "follow her bliss."

Pierre had taught Lara practically all she knew about joy and the pursuit of happiness. No one had ever spoken of bliss in her childhood home, where hard work was prized and happiness was found only in a job well done. Pierre had shown her how work and joy were compatible, and that both should have a place in one's life. And of course Pierre had given her a child who—no matter what the challenges of motherhood—had proved to be her greatest joy.

The first post-Pierre painting—the "feelings" painting—began to look like a great glow in the universe somewhere over a deep, turbulent sea. After some hours, she felt a need to connect the two areas—the glow and the murky depths—so she added a stream-like stroke between the two, gently curving it into the magenta swirl. By afternoon, Lara stepped back and thought, *Funny painting, this one, as if it came from way out there somewhere. I don't know this landscape, but it feels familiar. It looks like my own, after the earthquake hit.*

*

The next morning the sun blazed again around the window blinds, as it did morning after morning during that extraordinary May. Usually this part of the central coast would be under "May grey" cloudy skies, but it seemed that this spring the elements were conspiring to pull Lara and Henri out of bed earlier and earlier with a grand declaration: "Look! Life is good, life is beautiful. Look at the flowers, your green grass, the sky, and the birds. You cannot be sad now."

Today was supposed to be a second day to paint, and Lara looked forward to that, but first a few phone calls had to be made. Grizzly phone calls that no bear would ever make, that was for sure. An important event was fast approaching, and it was time Lara made some preparations, though her heart sank at the thought. Next month, she and Julie would fly to France where they would meet with Pierre's two sisters and his daughters from his first marriage. Together with some old friends they would scatter Pierre's ashes in the Mediterranean Sea.

Henri thought this was a strange idea and way too complicated. People made too much of beginnings and endings, he said; life itself was all a bear needed to celebrate. He was sure Pierre would not have liked the idea either, and Lara thought he was probably right. But the women closest to Pierre needed an experience of closure, and things were beginning to come together in a way that felt right. Pierre loved the Mediterranean where he once kept a boat, and a family friend had offered his house on the coast as a place for them all to stay.

Just one thing remained for Lara to clarify: the procedure for taking Pierre's ashes with her on the plane, and for taking them into France. She needed to talk to the French Consulate, to Air France and to the mortuary where the cremation had taken place, but she did not want to talk to any of them, nor did she even want to think about it. She sat down, pulled Henri into her lap, and began dialing.

In the end, all three places said some version of the same thing: put the box in checked luggage, along with paperwork stating where the cremation had taken place. "No problem," the husky-voiced mortuary man said. "We send people off on airplanes all the time. It shows up on the x-ray but the airlines know what it is."

Of course the French—being the French—had a much more elaborate but "optional" (legally speaking) idea of how things should be done. Lara sagged in her chair as the woman rattled off a list of necessary documents. She said Lara would need to bring the box to the French Consulate in Los Angeles, present the documents, pay thirty-five dollars, and have them seal the box. Henri read the dismay in her face and shook his head "No." Lara squeezed his paw in agreement and politely said goodbye. The official exporting of the ashes was an "option" she would skip.

The airline was mostly concerned with discretion. Urns, no matter how fancy, were not welcome in the passenger cabin. People were nervous enough about flying; they did not need to glimpse a reminder of mortality. Pierre's ashes would have to travel in the luggage compartment. Lara hung up the phone, leaned back in her chair and closed her eyes.

Her memory of the days after Pierre's death and cremation was hazy. Probably because of the shock. Although Lara had known for more than a year of her husbands life-threatening condition, he seemed so well and full of life that the end, when it came, was terribly sudden. Sometime after the cremation, the mortuary called to say that the package containing Pierre's remains was ready to be picked up, but Lara had no memory of that call. Two weeks went by before she finally contacted them and asked when she could collect the ashes. The simple truth was that she did not want to go.

When she finally did, Lara was presented with a white shopping bag containing a brown box, as if she were buying a pair of shoes. But this box was heavy, and it bore a label stating who was inside, now in his most compact form ever.

Lara had walked out of the mortuary, husband literally in hand, totally stunned. She was on her way to the department store to buy pillowcases, and she thought: *How can I write this in my diary?* "I picked up my husband's ashes in a little carrier bag and then went to buy pillow cases." *How can there be a day like this?* On the way home in the car, she had wanted more than anything to talk to him, to tell him about the surreal events of her day.

That car journey was six months ago, and the memory still pained her. Now she faced the prospect of a more demanding journey. She could hardly bear the thought of putting what was left of her husband into a suitcase to be rolled through airports, thrown into a cargo hold, and driven around in a car for weeks before reaching his last destination. Even if that destination was a carefully chosen, beautiful place, it seemed a bleak and lonely final journey for a man of such warmth and presence.

Henri did not have to ask what Lara was thinking; he saw the color drain from her face and he knew. He leaned his soft head into the sad curve of her body, and asked if it was true that there is a special lavender honey in Provence.

Lara blinked at him. "Lavender honey? Yes, they do. Why?"

Henri shrugged casually and said that he had been thinking he might like to go to France, too, especially if there was a delicious honey there that he had never tasted.

Lara nodded slowly, and Henri continued, suggesting that if he were going to make the trip, it seemed a good idea for him to ride in the luggage compartment, in the suitcase with Pierre. That way, he could wrap his arms around the box and its precious contents, and make sure it did not get jostled. He was just about to add that he was ideally suited for the task, being especially good at hugging, when Lara threw her arms around him and buried her face in his fur.

"Oh, yes, yes, Henri! Thank you, *merci!*"

They stayed like that for a while, then Henri reminded Lara that she had planned to paint again that day. So she went to her easel, took up her brushes and worked—not on the "feelings" painting, but on a small painting of an iris. She thought about the life and death of a flower, and of all of us, and how Henri was right: we humans make too much of beginnings and endings, when the whole cycle is equally important, and does not really ever stop or start in a single place. Lara found herself wishing she were an iris or a bear, more at ease in the cycle of life.

*

The sunny mornings continued. Sometimes the sunshine worked its magic so that Lara greeted the day with, if not joy, at least with determination. Then there were other days when Henri woke up severely crumpled from the intensity of Lara's embrace in the night and saw the old sadness and anxiety in her eyes.

He did not mind being squashed, if it helped her; he could feel her heartbeat steady and her muscles relax when she held him. But there was nothing Henri could do about the immense lonely flatness of a bed that used to slope downhill under the weight of the big French bear who had slept on the other side. He could not bring back the reassuring snores from a mate getting his rest, or the morning embrace that colored a whole day differently. Little Henri could not make up for that husband, so he did what he could: allow himself to be caught in an airless hug for hours on end.

This morning, Lara's sadness and anxiety sapped her energy, and she lay back hopelessly in her pillows, like an invalid.

Henri tried to remind her how fortunate she really was in the large scheme of things. For example, just yesterday, a curious long box had arrived in the mail. That in itself was exciting enough to Henri, who never received parcels, but inside this parcel was a bottle of *Champagne Brut Rosé*, sent straight from friends who produced Champagne in Hautvillers, France. No birthday or holiday had prompted this gift; it was simply a bubbly expression of love. How could Lara feel sad in the face of such a delightful event?

But this was one of those days when the reminder of her good fortune only made Lara feel worse, adding guilt to the mix of fear and melancholy she already carried. Someone who had so much to be grateful for should be doing more for other people who needed her! She wasn't doing enough for her aging parents; she wasn't supportive enough of her bereaved daughter; she should be exercising Lucie more; she should be exercising *herself* more! She could hardly remember the last time she had been down to the YMCA to swim.

Henri's ears pricked up at this. Finally, instead of talking about all the things she wasn't doing, Lara was talking about something that she could do, right now, to feel better. Lara had told him once that doing physical things helped her to calm down and stay in her body. Henri took her at her word on this— although, as a bear he never strayed from his body in the first place—and often told her to stop thinking and start moving.

So, in the middle of listing all the ways in which she was a failure, Lara felt a furry paw pressed firmly against her mouth, shushing her. This was followed by a polite suggestion that she get up and do something physical immediately (well, possibly after a bit of breakfast), although it did not have to involve a trip to the YMCA. Henri pointed out that if she threw the ball for Lucie she could exercise the dog and herself at the same time. He had no objection to swimming—though he himself never indulged—but he did think privately that swimming up and down long lanes of water in a hole in the ground was a peculiar form of exercise, especially for people who live right next to a perfectly good ocean.

Perhaps it was the shock of having her train of thought cut off so abruptly, but Lara did get up, and out they went into the sun. She set Henri down in a patch of lavender, and he watched her throw the ball for Lucie. With every joyous pounce and dash of the young dog's body, Henri saw Lara's own mood lift, until finally she was smiling. After that she walked the garden, greeting each lush and growing thing, pinching off shoots and smelling blossoms. He tried to be patient, knowing that to *breathe in the immensity of Nature* was part of her Tai Ji, but in the end he had to point out that it was long past time for breakfast. Always being present in his body, he reminded her, meant that he always knew how far he was from mealtime!

*

Over breakfast, Henri decided it was time to tackle the next big project on Lara's plate. He knew she did not want to think about it, but he also knew that putting off difficult tasks was a bad idea. He chose his moment perfectly, when a beam of sunlight shone on the honey pot just right, and turning it to liquid gold. Then he asked casually when Lara was planning to pack up the stuff in her old art studio.

She looked at him in dismay.

Henri carried on as if he hadn't noticed her reaction, pointing out that in fact *right now* would be a good time to start, while honey calories would give them energy to work.

Lara did not look as though right now would be a good time. She looked as though he had asked her to pack her bags and go off to war.

She knew the task had to be done sometime: she needed to give up her art studio downtown and create one at home. The studio was on a noisy, dirty street; here at home she could enjoy the garden, and have Lucie and Henri around her. Also, she could stop paying double utilities on everything. This change made sense, but it added to her general feeling of disorientation: things were not as they used to be. And that disorientation added, in turn, to the loss of confidence she felt without Pierre, who had been her biggest fan.

Henri thought it was enough just to be Lara, like he was Henri. Why was there all this fuss about achievement and what others expected? Henri knew Lara was a good person. He could tell by how she never forgot to get out his honey pot, how she made the garden so beautiful, and how she cooked meals people exclaimed about. Her paintings were full of color and gave views to rooms that had none. People were always calling, inviting her to things, and sending her mail from around the world. Henri thought she had one of the best lives he'd ever heard of and he was so happy to live with her. He vowed to keep her on track and chase away all the doubt, fear, guilt and anxiety she inexplicably carried.

"I don't think I can face the studio today, Henri," she said.

He pondered this for a moment. Sometimes in situations like this he would recommend a nap, but he knew that time was growing short before their upcoming trip to France, and he knew that Lara would feel much better when this was done. In a burst of uncharacteristic bravado, Henri climbed up on the breakfast table, stood before Lara's teacup and told her to go and put on her jeans, because this task was going to get done today! For heaven's sake, she was not moving to Siberia; once she got started it would not be so hard. *You can do this!* he insisted.

Something about this sudden decisiveness, coming from the gentle bear who had hugged her all night, broke through Lara's fog of inertia. She got dressed, put some empty boxes in the car, and off they went. As they drove along, Henri hummed cheerfully to himself: "Just whistle while you work, ta ta da da ta ta ta . . ." He was a hopeless Disney fan.

Lara shook her head and smiled. Henri's charm never ceased to bamboozle her, and she thought once more to herself that she would be happier if she could just see things the way he did. Regarding this change in life, for instance: the trick was to see it as a fork in the road, a continuation of her life down a different path, rather than a brutal ending. Her melancholy perspective, by contrast, could turn ordinary life experiences into a Wagnerian tragedy. She knew it would take time—and a lot more of Henri's pep talks—to change that.

Perhaps it was the effect of Henri's humming, but by the time they got to the studio, Lara was ready to get to work. She started sorting and packing, and for every problem that arose, Henri had a positive solution. Sell some of the furniture through a consignment shop. Give some to friends who could use it. The more ideas he had, the more elated he got, and he never tired of cheering her on: Go, Lara!

She would laugh and empty another drawer thinking, yes, *I will find homes for all this stuff.* Recycling was a passion of hers, so this was the perfect task for her. The main thing was not to bring it all home. Definitely not.

Henri was exhausted by mid afternoon, but the color had come back to Lara's face, and the move was in progress. He decided it was worth missing a nap for that.

That night they both slept well. Before they fell asleep, Lara told Henri she could never have tackled the move without him. He smiled his bear smile and drifted off into his usual dream, one of endless trees full of honeycombs. Lara dreamed of painting large oil paintings again, and listening to birds on the patio instead of the traffic on the street by the old studio. In her dream, Lucie slept by the easel and music played. A new landscape burst forth on the white canvas.

*

On a June morning, in France, a white cloud spread out against the blue green sea, gently swirling and forming different shapes as it mingled with the salt water. Lara's husband's ashes began to draw their own picture, almost a body's form at first, like a ghost, then widening into a heart shape, then dispersing, falling deeper into the sea.

Stunned, Lara asked herself, *How could my 220 pound, six-and-a-half-feet tall husband be dissolved in the sea like that? How could I throw him there?* A wave of nausea came over her and she had to sit down as the boat moved gently back and forth on the calm welcoming sea. Lara, her daughter and the rest of Pierre's family did what they had intended to do: they returned Pierre to his own country and to nature, through the waters of his favorite sea—the Mediterranean. But the intention did not forsee how it felt to actually do it.

Lara sat off to one side, her body curled against the nausea and grief that threatened to overwhelm her. The others tossed hundreds of flower tops onto the sea where the white ghost had been. Soon only the happy-colored flowers were visible, floating gently. *Where did he go?* Eight sad people stood in awe on the two little fishing boats, rocking, waiting, watching the bright flowers make a long blanket in magenta, orange, yellow and white.

Once Lara dared to look again, she took up her camera to capture what was happening. It was in her blood to document anything of importance or extraordinary beauty; she couldn't help it, even now. Then she, too, threw the rest of the blossoms in the direction of her last sighting of Pierre.

The whole scene felt unreal. It was a fine sunny day in the south of France, a slight breeze carried the scent of the sea, and she parted from her husband literally, physically, for the last time in a spot offshore between Toulon and Marseilles. Where would he travel? How could a body transform so much? The circumstances felt strange and somewhat contrived. The family had felt they must do something—something together to mark the finality of this man they had all lost. And so they had, they had witnessed this moment together, but the only thing that felt real was still the loss, the utter and complete loss.

After some time, someone suggested that the borrowed boats needed to be returned. The silence was broken by the "chug-chug" of the motors starting up, and Lara and the seven other mourners watched the carpet of flowers recede into the distance. Lara and Julie cried at leaving Pierre truly for the last time. Both resisted an impulse to wave farewell at the carpet of flowers, feeling awkward in front of the others. They held each other's shoulders; that was all.

Julie said she felt better, and even smiled. Yet Lara felt as sad as the day Pierre had died. It all came back to her . . . the immense loss . . . missing the person who shared half of her life. She was exhausted, had no idea what time it was, and hardly knew where she was, as they alighted from the boats in the harbor.

The sun was blazing; Lara was wearing a borrowed sunhat

that was too small. Everything was a blur. Standing with the bewildered group of mourners on the quay with their empty flower baskets and wounded hearts, Lara tried to come back to the present. Although she had no appetite, it was time to resume the role of hostess to those who would want lunch before their TGV train trip back to Paris. Still, she had no money with her, and no desire to go to a noisy restaurant on such an extraordinary day.

Sophie, Pierre's daughter, who was just three years younger than Lara herself, came over and gave her a kiss on the cheek, gently saying she thought their goodbye had gone well, that it was beautiful. In fear of breaking down again, Lara replied, "How about we go buy some fresh fish? Do you have any money on you?"

They decided to go to the fishmonger just a little way down the quay, where they agreed on the *dorade*, caught that morning off that very coast. As they walked back to the house, the smell of the sea went with them, mingling first with the scent of the hot pine needles lining the street, then with the smell of eucalyptus in the forest, until they arrived at the house overlooking the water. Lara looked down at the sparkling blue expanse, knowing that it now included Pierre and all the flowers they had thrown.

Sophie set to work preparing the fish for the oven, while Lara cut the succulent ripe melons, and others set the long table under the parasol pines in the back yard, out of the wind. Soon all seven women were eating, laughing and making toasts to Pierre, his life, and being together. Though he was not there, Pierre had brought what was left of his family together in a place he would have loved.

After lunch, they clambered down steep stairs to a little rocky inlet, and all of them together—the fifty-plus-year-old women and their daughters—swam in the clear water, taking turns floating in the inner tubes, giggling like children, splashing, screaming, swimming some more, and finally baking their bodies in the sun.

*

The Air France flight was packed—jammed in with Americans heading home, and a few French people going to Tahiti—yet Lara felt very much on her own. Henri was in her checked luggage, and Julie stayed behind to spend another month in France to soak up its culture, sights, food, friends and relatives, and, of course, *le français*. Lara smiled at the memory of their last conversation: already Julie sounded just like a French person...just like her father.

It had been twenty-four years since Lara had taken this flight alone. She missed Pierre, she missed Julie, and yet there was a certain peace about being on her own now. Pierre had gone home to France, which felt right: he was closer to his blood relatives, back in his beloved Mediterranean. Again, Lara admired her daughter's innate wisdom in suggesting the idea. As hard as it had been to hold her husband in her hands in the form of ashes, and then to let him go, Lara had accepted and fulfilled the task for Julie's sake, and in the end it had proved cathartic.

Perhaps, Lara thought, this would set them both on a new course in life: less afraid, more courageous.

It felt strange to return to an empty house. Lucie was there to greet her, and that helped: her ebullient welcome banished the echoing silence. It also helped to see Henri's familiar round shape when she opened her suitcase. Henri was a little out of sorts, and announced firmly that he would like to go on a *more fun* trip next time. Lara hugged him tightly, and they both felt a little better.

After a cup of tea, they sat at Lara's computer and looked

through all the photos of the trip on the screen. The first picture was of Henri in the car, and he grumbled that he didn't need a picture to remind him of all the long, hot drives he had endured, but then came pictures of Henri nestled in red poppies, and Henri in a field of lavender, and Henri at Versailles, and he admitted that some of their outings had been quite pleasant.

"And you're such a cultured bear now!" Lara reminded him. Henri said he supposed he was, but would have preferred more honey tasting *dégustation*.

Then came pictures of Henri's visits with family members where hugs were plentiful, as others who mourned Pierre's loss also discovered that hugging a furry bear can ease the pain a little.

"What a good job you did there, Henri," said Lara, "So many hugs were needed."

Henri went quiet, and then, in a small voice, admitted that he really was glad he had gone along.

But he would still like a more fun trip next time.

*

When Lara woke up the next morning, after coming home and she could not think of a reason to get up. It was not that she felt particularly sad or anxious; she just felt aimless. Apart from watching over her aging parents, what was this next phase of her life going to be about? Henri nudged her out of bed, and reminded her that her life *right now* should be about putting her feet on the floor and finding some breakfast. There would be plenty of time after that, he said, for them to discuss anything more challenging.

"Something more challenging," mused Lara, over her cup of tea. "That may be what I need. But not the kind of challenge my everyday life feels like right now, when my main job is driving all over town and remembering my parents' appointments; that wears me down."

Henri nodded emphatically: Lara most definitely did not need any more wearing down. If there was a challenge out there that could do exactly the opposite, then that was what she needed.

She started thinking out loud: "It should be something completely new to me, exciting, even a little scary—I need to be able to feel a sense of accomplishment."

Lara remembered the thoughts she had had on the plane coming home from France: *facing one challenge makes the next challenge less frightening, and puts us on a more courageous path*. She closed her eyes and saw herself back on the little boat in the Mediterranean. In that moment, she had faced her fears, and had done the very thing she did not want to do: hold Pierre's ashes, and then let them spill from her hands into the clear blue sea.

The sea. Now that it had come to mind, it stayed; all day, as Lara went about her routines, she thought about it. The Mediterranean had been so clear and clean, so blue, so full of fish, with such pure winds. The ocean in Santa Barbara was different, but had its own beauty and was close by, accessible. Pierre had loved sailing and he and Lara had gone out on friends' boats now and then. A long-standing fear of the sea had kept Lara from learning to sail, and so—unable to participate—she often ended up feeling like a bump on a log.

But although she still felt some of that old fear, her feelings about the sea now were so much deeper. She was drawn to its eternal vastnessand to the feeling of freedom that sailing offered, harnessing as it did the limitless powers of wind and current. And she was drawn to an image of herself in which she navigated a new course for her life by mastering a new skill.

By the end of the day she decided to at least explore the

possibility of learning to sail. Henri was doubtful, but as always, he approved of anything that brought a sparkle to Lara's eyes. She began by phoning some boating friends, and asking if they would teach her to crew for them. One friend had a better idea. "Why don't you take lessons at the Sailing Center?" she suggested. "Then you'd get a good grounding in the whole subject and learn much more than I could ever teach you—more than I probably know myself!"

Two days later, Lara took an introductory ride on a J24 (a twenty-four-foot keel boat) with a Center instructor and other prospective students. One of the students was very careful where he sat, and talked about a friend who had been struck dead by the boom coming across fast and hard into his head. In a matter of seconds, he said, his friend's wife had become a widow at only forty-two, while out on a "pleasure" boat.

Lara squirmed, shifting away from the boom. What the heck was she doing in this boat anyway? It was all very well for Henri to chat about challenges. He was at home taking a nap! Still, she was determined to continue. Just being alive was risky; she knew that now. She had lost Pierre already, what else did she have to lose? She had begun to feel that everything seemed less intense, less important, as she got older. Perhaps a new flexibility was waiting in the sails.

After the introductory session, Lara's only hesitation about sailing was that she didn't want to sign up for lessons alone, so she was delighted when Toni, a member of her women's writing group, said she'd be interested, too. A few days later, the two of them stepped onto a J24 with their instructor, Trudy. After an hour or so of learning about the rigging and some basic knots, Trudy backed them out of the slip. Soon they headed smoothly out of the harbor and into the Channel. At that point, everything changed.

It was far windier that day than it had been on the introductory ride. Within moments the boat tipped on its side, its sails filling with an impressive wind. Lara's stomach flopped, and she held on tight as they raced across the water. Just as swiftly, serious doubts swelled in Lara's mind. *I must be crazy*, she thought, squinting into the seaspray. *How is it possible to learn* anything *at breakneck speed, heeled over and just barely hanging on?*

That first four-hour lesson was rough. Toni was the bold one, taking the helm for over an hour. Lara worked the jib without much understanding. By the next day, though, some of the vocabulary had sunk in and Lara and Toni were back for more. They had hoped to stay out of the heavy wind, and would have been content to practice docking all day, but Trudy got them out into the Channel again, and this time they took turns at the helm.

They sailed back into the harbor with Lara at the helm. While tacking carefully, to avoid hitting any of the other boats, she had an epiphany. <u>This</u> *is what I always try to avoid: being in the position of true responsibility, the one having to make critical decisions by myself.* She realized she had not enjoyed being the one doing all the driving in France—she so missed Pierre's confident ease in that role. *The helm is exactly where I don't want to be!* she thought, flinching as they skimmed past the gleaming hulls of millionaires' yachts.

After that second day's lesson, Lara wobbled home on her sea legs, exhausted. Henri was waiting at the door to greet her with a hug.

"Remember when I said my life was wearing me down, Henri?" she groaned, sinking into a chair. "Well, now it's wearing me *out!* And I'm still not sure when this is going to be fun." Henri made sympathetic noises, and added that bears never go out on boats. One good reason why: there is no honey to be found at sea.

Finally, by the fourth day of the sailing course, Lara began to get the feel of the tiller and a reliable sense of which way to push or pull, to go where she wanted. She passed the test by bringing the boat into the dock without using the motor—and without putting a single scratch on its hull. She felt a rush of pride.

Her fear of the sea had transformed into a healthy respect, and had incidentally prompted her to make a personal vow to never go out in winds above 12 knots. She felt the results of her week on the water, and not just in her muscles. She had concentrated so hard on learning new skills, new knots, and even a new language, that she had given her brain a total vacation from personal worries. The big daily dose of oxygen and ions off the water had given her the best sleep she'd had in months. And best of all, she had accomplished something that she had once thought was too hard, and in so doing had opened the door to a new chapter in her life.

Lara's proudest day was when she received a certificate, entitling her to rent and sail a boat of equivalent size anywhere in the world. Henri suggested that she place the certificate on the mantel next to a photograph of a smiling Pierre. It seemed just right. *He would be wearing just that smile if he were here to see this,* she thought. She turned to Henri.

"Now, shall we celebrate with champagne? Or should we open one of the fancy pots of honey?" The look on Henri's face made it clear that there was no contest. Honey it was, straight from the pot. That must have put him in an unusually fine mood, because later he asked if it was possible to get life-jackets in his size. Now that Lara had her permit (and as long as a supply of honey could be brought along) Henri thought he might be willing to give sailing a try himself.

*

Sometimes, during the heat of that summer, Lara woke up damp with sweat. At first she thought it might be a lingering effect of menopause, but soon she realized that her skin was sweaty only where she had been holding Henri against her body. Wise and cheerful he may be, she thought wryly, but he was also made of modern fibers—lightweight, but very warm. On these hot nights she would have to remember to hold just one paw, like she used to do sometimes with Pierre.

Even on the warmest nights, she wished Pierre's head was resting on the pillow next to hers. During the last year before his death, Pierre had wondered now and then if he should move to another bed for her sake: his snoring might be too loud, or his search for a comfortable position for his aching joints would move the whole mattress and tug at the sheets. But Lara always refused the idea. They were married, and the disruptions of a shared bed came with the territory. Two bears in one cave, one bed.

Lara felt his absence daily, in her very skin. She had lost not just his wonderful mind, not just his love and wisdom and *joie de vivre*, she had lost *him*, the simple, tangible presence of his body. She missed the friendly snuggle while watching a movie on the couch, the unexpected hug while she was doing the dishes. Without his familiar loving touch, daily life took on a coolness, an aloneness, that made her sad. She made a point of giving and grabbing a hug when she saw Julie or a close friend, but those moments were rare, and they were not the same. And Henri— well, Henri was always there, and he did his best, but even he knew that he was no substitute for the big bear he had never met.

Then one day a friend gave Lara a gift certificate for a massage. She had never had a professional, paid-for massage in her life; that sort of thing simply had not been done in her family, and would have been regarded as an extravagance. But a few days later, Lara lay on a comfortable, heated table at the massage studio, and was amazed by how good it felt to be rubbed all over by warm, caring hands. In addition to all the physical benefits the masseuse touted—the increased circulation, the balancing of the lymph flow throughout the body—Lara left the studio with a new sense of well-being that she knew came simply from the benefit of touch. It was a welcome feeling after her lengthy solitude. The problem was the cost: without Pierre's income, she was trying to cut back on all expenses. Perhaps this was not the time for massage.

Then came a moment of synchronicity.

Lara often offered a ride to Kathleen, a gifted poet, when she attended a local poetry workshop. Kathleen suffered from multiple sclerosis and used a walker, but she never complained about her situation. As the two women chatted in the car one day, Kathleen announced that a young woman was now living in her guest apartment in exchange for massages several times a week. Her doctor had recommended massage for her beleaguered limbs, and she felt it was doing her a lot of good, both physically and mentally. Lara's ears perked up. Kathleen also mentioned that Monique, the masseuse, often takes her folding table with her to make house calls, and that Lara might benefit from this woman's skill. *This sounds promising*, Lara thought.

"Oh, and Monique is Swiss," added Kathleen, as the car reached her house. "She speaks French." That settled it: Lara took Monique's phone number before helping Kathleen into her house. As she drove home, she thought again of the courage and grace with which Kathleen faced her illness, and was reminded that she should be more grateful for the physical health she took for granted. There was no excuse for feeling sorry for herself.

When she got home, Henri was sitting on the kitchen table, ready for lunch. While Lara moved around the room preparing the meal, Henri mentioned that she looked better, more alive, than when she left that morning. He knew she always liked her poetry workshop. It was a place where she was free to speak her heart honestly. Other widows in the group understood; they had all done their share of grieving. But apparently it wasn't the workshop that excited Lara; it was someone named Monique, who could give a massage and speak French at the same time. Henri was not entirely sure what a massage was, but anything that made Lara look so alive had to be a good thing. As soon as lunch was over he told Lara to call the amazing Monique. So Lara called, and immediately warmed to the positive, cheerful voice that greeted her. Monique had recently completed her training, and the price she quoted was one Lara thought she could manage. Better still, Monique would come to the house. Lara would be more relaxed there, and could stay that way, without having to dress again in street clothes and drive home.

Lara talked it over with Henri. She explained how good a massage made her feel, but that it was a little expensive. Henri felt a bit miffed that she had found something that worked better than his hugs, but Lara misunderstood his silence. "This is self-indulgent, isn't it?" she asked. "It's too much money."

Instantly, Henri forgot the insult to his hugs, and worked to reassure her. He pointed out all the ways that she was saving money: she had cancelled the paper, she wasn't renting the studio downtown anymore, and her grocery bill was smaller these days. That was more than enough to compensate for something that she found so helpful.

Looking happier again, Lara asked, "So...shall we give it a try?" Henri said that in his considered opinion it was an excellent plan, and she planted a kiss on his big, fat nose.

So Lara started to have a massage once a week. Monique would bring CDs of soothing music—soft jazz, guitar, harp—and organic essential oils, that added the marvelous fragrances of lavender, rose and geranium to the experience. Her touch was both gentle and firm, and her voice soft. As the two women chatted in French, Lara felt somehow close to Pierre. Before long, Lara was converted: this was not a luxury, but a necessity. With the calm that she experienced, even after a troublesome day dealing with the logistics of her parents' care, she felt once again that she could cope. Most of all, during each massage, she felt centered in her own body and grateful to be there. All was as it should be.

*

That August, when Lara was in the ninth month of widowhood, she became more and more aware of her dreams. Until now it seemed they were hiding, or perhaps the sleeping aids she took kept them underground. But lately, Lara had begun to feel more alive, and—perhaps due to the challenge of learning to sail—to value alertness and mental precision more than the numbness to pain that sleep medication gave her. She cut the dosage, then stopped them entirely, and her reward came in dreams. Big, elaborate dreams.

In one dream, Lara found herself in the narrow cobblestone streets of a European city. Longing to explore its ancient mystery, she found herself trying to persuade a man to join her. Even in the dream, she knew she was being pulled back to the belief that she needed a man with her before she could explore. Finally she struck out on her own, only to realize that she had forgotten her baby somewhere, and needed to find it.

In the morning, she told Henri about it and he shook his head in amazement, wondering how she could get any rest at all during such an exhausting dream. He would need twice as many naps if his dreams were that busy!

"But what do you think it all meant?" she asked. He puzzled over that while she put the bread in the toaster. Finally he said that, though he really did not know much about dreams, it sounded as if Lara was curious to get out into the world, but still felt scared of being on her own, and that she was worried about losing Julie altogether, once she moved out.

Lara stared at him, wide-eyed. "Wow, for a stuffed bear, you make a pretty good analyst." Henri didn't respond, not being completely sure what an analyst might be. "But you didn't say anything about the mysterious man," prompted Lara. Henri shrugged and said that he had no idea who the man might be. What did he look like?

Lara laughed. "He looked like Ben Affleck, which was fun. I saw him in *People* magazine in the waiting room at Dad's eye doctor appointment yesterday. I guess I just reused his nice face." Then the toast popped, and they had their breakfast. Henri smiled as he licked a stray drop of honey from his spoon. It was good to hear Lara laugh.

That night, Lara seemed restless as she slept, and at one point she squeezed Henri so tightly that he squeaked. But he didn't mind; he just snuggled in closer and murmured in her ear: *You don't need to be afraid, Lara. You'll see. You are waking up now, like from a long, sad nightmare. Your life is changed, but you are okay. You are still you.*

A few days later Lara woke from a different kind of dream; in it she was at a huge Easter feast in a gigantic home somewhere, and she was sorting through and organizing napkins that were beautifully hand-embroidered with many different names and flowers. A feeling of immensity and abundance pervaded her being. In that dream she had a purpose.

That morning felt like a new start. She went for a sail. Life had changed, but she was still okay.

*

Late August finally felt like summer, with rising temperatures and lots of sun. Lara relished this period of light and tried not to think about the coming fall, when the days would grow short and she would approach the November anniversary of Pierre's death. She tried not to dwell on the past or the future, and on many days she succeeded, but some days there would be moments when she could not shake the sadness, could not escape the longing to have Pierre back in her life.

Henri would try to pull her out of it, to distract her or cheer her up, or even to give her a little push when she needed it to get outside into the fresh air or to pick up her paintbrush. She had come so far: building new routines, planting the grapevine, moving out of her studio, taking Pierre back to France, and learning to sail, but on some days she was still just plain sad, all day long.

Henri sighed. He was running out of ideas. Then it hit him: Lara often felt better after writing to Christine in France. Why didn't she write a letter to Pierre?

Lara looked at him, confused. "What do you mean write to him?"

It was hard for Henri to explain: he was remembering all the times she had wished she could say things to Pierre, even though it was too late to do so. Maybe those thoughts needed to find their way out of her head and onto the page. Maybe it didn't matter whether the letter ever got mailed. In the end, Henri simply pushed a yellow legal pad and a pen across the table. *Just write.*

The clock ticked. Lara frowned. Finally, she poured herself another cup of tea, and picked up the pen.

Dear Pierre,

    I am trying to live without you. After twenty-three years together, it feels so unnatural.

    I know you did not want to go, but I also know that you were fed up with your aging body, suffering physically a lot of the time. I can understand that it was time to go, I can even accept it. But without you, daily life feels so awkward, and my need to talk to you is greater than my reason, which says that you are gone forever.

    I want to tell you that I listen to you now, even more than when I had you with me. During all our years in France, and while we were raising Julie, you always thought I was just rushing by, not listening, not noticing your point of view, because I would seem contrary, or surer of myself than I was.

    But I can still hear you, and now I admit you were often right. It's funny: the bear Julie gave me sounds like you sometimes. You always said, 'Are you here, <u>now</u>? Be present, and pay attention!' It is the sort of thing Henri says. I gave him your middle name to honor you, because it's him I sleep with now, in the bed that used to be just right for six-and-a-half feet of you and five-feet-nine inches of me. Henri can't fill that space, but he is good company, and better than an empty bed.

    The garden misses you too. It's not what it used to be with your careful watering, feeding and gopher patrol. And the kitchen…it never smells of long-cooked Pot-au-Feu or fresh strawberry confiture anymore. As for me, Pierre, I so miss hearing your soothing French voice. I wish I had recorded all the songs you used to sing to Julie, the poems you used to recite, the recipes you got over the phone from your sister.

You were France for me. By living with you I felt I was still there. I don't feel that way anymore. I have to go looking for it—seek out French people to talk to, read Le Monde, *watch the French news on TV. Before, you brought it all to me in your voice.*

Lara paused, leaned her chin on one hand and gazed into space. Then she turned, and caught a questioning look from Henri. She shook her head.

"No, Henri, I'm not done. I think I am just in the middle. You'd better go have your morning nap, and I'll wake you when I'm finished. Now you've got me started, there is so much I want to say." Henri sighed, and Lara smiled: "Hey, this was your idea, remember?" Then she flipped the yellow paper to another sheet, took a sip of cold tea and continued:

I miss your warm body beside me all night. I miss your desire to make love with me, even though it annoyed me sometimes. I wish that I had played more and worked less—and worried less—like you. I was raised to believe that life is work, and that I was supposed to accomplish something of note. Now I know that I won't—things like that don't usually happen to people who are almost sixty.

You had the joie de vivre—*you lived in the moment, engaging with what was in front of you. You didn't waste time seeking after uncertainties or keeping possibilities for later, a later that might never come. You spent your life fully, spent your money generously with all the people who were precious to you. I liked your style.*

I want to be like that, but I feel as though I am, as sailors say, 'in irons.' I am headed straight into the wind, can

42

feel it coming hard onto my face, but my sails are luffing, limp
or swinging, going nowhere. My boat is stalled, waiting for
something inside me to change, something that will move the
sails enough to get me out of 'irons,' out of a prison that does not
have to exist. On a bad day I just want to follow you into death
and stop trying to figure out how to proceed in life.

I miss you.

My letter to you is not finished but Henri is up from his
nap (unusually brief, for him!) and whispering to me that I am
missing a wonderful summer day, and should get out there
before it is gone. I will finish my letter tomorrow. Mainly I
want you to know that I still hear you and wish you could take
pleasure in what you still mean to me.

Bye for now,

Lara

*

September opened with dire earthquake predictions in California and hurricane warnings in Florida. Nature seemed to be acting up, or out. In the foothills of the Santa Ynez Mountains, the winds were dry, bringing no rain.

One morning, while walking with Henri in the garden, Lara stopped and looked around, as if seeing things clearly for the first time in weeks. "Oh, Henri! Look how dry it is! How did this happen?" Henri started to say something about how plants do tend to dry up without water, but then he saw that Lara was trying hard not to cry, so he stopped.

Lara was remembering: it was Pierre who always watered the garden. She could see him in her mind's eye, as she had seen him on so many days: watering the lavender, the roses, the Bird of

Paradise—the hummingbird's favorite snack bar. He would take pleasure watching the spray fall to where it was needed, and washing the freeway dust off the glossy leaves of the shrubs.

Now those leaves were covered in dust, and Lara hated to see it. Just one more reminder that there was no Pierre. She could not keep up all the watering, not if she wanted to do anything else. She could manage the backyard, and loved to be able to see that little green oasis from the windows, but how much money would it cost to get help with the rest?

She discussed it with Henri over breakfast, and after some honey-fueled pondering, Henri suggested that it might be good to let the some of the yard go back to what it used to be, here in this drought-prone part of the world.

"You mean desert landscaping?" Lara considered this. "I was wondering about that too…boulders and gravel and cactus…it can look very nice. And with no watering; I'd like that! We could try it in the side yard. I'm not sure how Lucie will take to it, though. She spends a lot of time there."

Henri knew why: Lucie loved to run alongside the joggers who passed the fence. He suspected, however, that she would run and bark just as happily on gravel as she did on grass, and the dust she kicked up wouldn't bother a few desert boulders. He said he was sure Lucie would approve, and congratulated Lara on another splendid idea.

"Was it my idea?" smiled Lara. "Sometimes I'm not sure whether you think of these things first, or I do."

This business of having to make decisions without Pierre was another change in her landscape, and it was taking some getting used to. Lara felt embarrassed, at fifty-seven, having such trouble making decisions. Often she just pretended to know what to do, so it was good to have Henri's listening ear. When she talked to him, it felt as though she could work her way towards the wisest course of action.

The biggest, best decision of late was converting the garage into a studio space: freshly dry-walled and painted, white, high-ceilinged. No more smelly oil and turpentine wafting into the bedroom and discouraging deep breathing during yoga time. Lucie could wander in and out of the garden and visit Lara painting; the new Dutch door stood open, and a breeze drifted through from the new window on the side. A skylight had been added as well. All of this had been accomplished in ten days by an extraordinary crew of men who worked from dawn to dark to finish the job quickly.

Henri could feel the change in Lara's mood. She was excited about moving into her new space. Energy flowed again in a nice way. She got up eagerly in the mornings, and started thinking about new paintings.

"You know, Henri, I have come back to where I began. When I attended U.C. Berkeley I lived in a two-room triplex that had a garage, and that's where I set up my painting gear and produced a lot of work. I sold it off the walls of various restaurants around town, and made some cash that way."

Henri did not seem surprised. He could imagine Lara as a young, spirited artist, and glimpsed that person in her now. As far as he was concerned, the decision to work at home worked splendidly, as he could enjoy long, peaceful days in the studio while Lara painted and Lucie raised dust. In his opinion a little music might be nice out there, too, but Lara said she was not sure about that yet. Generally, she preferred silence, but she was open to the possibility of change. Henri nodded, and thought to himself: *Lara is going to be all right.*

*

Most mornings still started with an email from Christine in France, but there was a change in the wind on that front as well. After more than two years of widowhood, Christine had met a man. Her messages had taken on the excitement of soap opera installments: "Will he ask me out? What will I wear? God, my feet are a mess! When will he kiss me?" Lara was equally excited to open the emails: it felt as though they were both seventeen again.

What a change from the torment of the last few years for Christine! She had met the new man, Bernard, while out collecting mushrooms near a small country road, her dogs with her. He stopped his car and started asking about the mushrooms, showing his own knowledge on the subject, and about dogs—his own was bouncing on the seat behind him. To her amazement he invited her to dinner at his house for the next day.

At first Christine had decided Bernard must be gay because he was so concerned with the details of things and was passionate about cooking, and his home and garden. Christine wrote, "I don't trust my own judgment about this guy. I think I will invite him to meet my sons when they are around, to get their reactions."

Lara read the emails with a vicarious thrill. At the same time, she realized how utterly dead she felt in that area of her own life. She still felt completely married, wore her ring, never thought about men at all, and did not miss sex. It was as if she had been in limbo since the day Pierre died; all her feelings from before that day were frozen in time, unchanged even by nine months without him.

Christine was so excited: "When Bernard went to Paris yesterday, I found myself waiting for a phone call, my stomach fluttering when he did call. I think about him all the time. What is happening to me?"

Lara smiled. It seemed obvious what was happening, and it was quaintly naïve that her friend should pose the question. But, like Lara, Christine had been with her husband twenty-three years. She had forgotten how the first days of a new relationship felt, when one couldn't think about anything else. It was wonderful to hear her friend so happy all of a sudden.

Henri peered at the computer screen, to see what was making Lara cry out "Bravo!" all by herself. After reading along for a while, he became quite interested in the whole story, and said that he thought it was a good sign that this man could cook...but it would be even better if it turned out he also kept bees.

Lara smiled. "I'll tell Christine to find out," she said. But while she typed, a selfish thought occurred to her. If Christine did fall in love with Bernard, she wouldn't need Lara's constant email companionship anymore. One of them would be getting back to a man/woman relationship and sharing her days' events with him instead of her old friend.

Ah, well, she thought. *Life changes. It keeps on changing, and I just may change too.*

*

Although the weather continued to be hot and dry, autumn arrived, and Lara was aware that before the season was over she would have to face the first anniversary of Pierre's death. Before then, she wanted some time away from Santa Barbara, where reminders of Pierre were everywhere. She wondered about going to visit her cousin Angela. The two had grown up near each other in California, but now Angela lived in Massachusetts. The more Lara thought about it, the more a New England fall sounded ideal: a chance to reconnect with family, and a chance to drink in new sights, smells and sounds.

Henri was not thrilled at the prospect of another trip. He said he had heard New Englanders didn't eat honey, preferring something called maple syrup! He wrinkled his nose in disgust.

Lara scratched him reassuringly behind the ears. "Don't worry, Henri," she said. "Of course there will be honey. And beautiful trees, like you've never seen, and no long, hot drives like in France. This trip will be fun!"

Henri was still skeptical: how could Lara know that for sure?

"How?" Lara laughed. "Because *you'll* be there! It wouldn't be much fun without you, even if you are grumpy."

Well, when she put it that way, thought Henri, it was hard to disagree.

And from the start, this trip did feel very different from the last one. For all its moments of beauty and joy, the journey to France was taken in order to accomplish a sad task, and it had left Lara exhausted. This journey, she hoped, would leave her rested and energized. With that aim, and adopting the axiom "Love thyself," she used her frequent flyer miles to award herself the grand luxury of an upgrade to business class. What fun to eat on real china! To drink from a real glass, have real linens and real silverware—except for the knife, of course, which was pale blue plastic. Even in business class, she wasn't allowed to forget that she lived in post-9/11 world.

The moment Lara lifted Henri out of his suitcase in the third-floor guestroom at Angela's house in Cambridge, he could tell she was happier. She plopped him down on the windowsill, and together they looked down at the trees below. He felt a bit dizzy—it was a whole new perspective for a small bear, gazing down through the branches from above—but Lara held him steady, and pointed out the many vivid colors in the turning leaves.

"Isn't it amazing?" she asked, and he agreed, his gaze following the squirrels as they leapt from branch to branch.

After Lara unpacked, they headed downstairs for dinner. The enormous old Victorian house had spectacular woodwork everywhere, and two huge staircases, with smooth, shining wood handrails for Henri to slide down. Lara wasn't sure he would enjoy that, since the slide ended with a bump, but after his first try, Henri announced that he would like another go. Lara looked back up the long staircase and shook her head.

"You can slide when we're going down," she said. "Getting back up again is a different matter. I'll be getting my cardiac workout while we're here." She dropped her voice: "And God forbid I have to go to the bathroom in the night. There isn't one on our floor."

As always, Henri thought how glad he was to be a stuffed bear who never needed to worry about such things. And when they sat down at the dining table—Lara's grandmother's table—Henri was relieved to see that he also would not need to worry about honey: there was a jar and spoon laid out just for him. Lara seemed happy, too, and told him that they were eating off of her grandmother's special plates.

"Look at these chairs!" she exclaimed, gently running her hand across the beautiful needlepoint designs that covered each one. "Oma did all this, Henri. I remember watching her stitch when I was a little girl."

Angela and Lara began to talk, and over the next few days they talked on and on, their conversations weaving around shared memories. They looked at photographs and told stories. When Lara saw the blue and white Chinese rugs in the living room, she felt like she was five again, playing on the floor at Oma's, feeling the dense wool under her bare knees. Visiting Angela was a voyage back to childhood.

On the last day in Massachusetts, they went for a long walk. At first, Henri didn't want to go. He was snuggled comfortably under the bedcovers. He told Lara that the autumn weather made him want to try hibernating, like the local bears. But in the end, Lara persuaded him to come along, and it was a beautiful day: the sky a clear blue, the air crisp but not cold. When they stopped to rest, Lara and Angela sat on a bench, and Henri found himself up to his ears in a large pile of wildly colorful leaves. He looked at Lara and saw a new lightness in her face. All her worries were a long way away. He lay back amidst the rustling layers of gold and red, and thought that there was quite a lot to be said for traveling, after all.

*

On an October morning, just a few weeks after returning from New England, Lara and Henri set off in the car on a much shorter trip. Just a few hours up the California coast, on the edge of Morro Bay, Lara was going to attend a seminar in Tai Ji.

She liked learning the gracious, slow movements, all having to do with sky, fire, water, wood, and tigers, and she felt grateful for the opportunity to practice those movements in a place where the elements were so vividly present—except for the tigers, of course. Lara was especially excited, though, to see another form of wildlife for which the bay was known: sea otters.

She held sea otters and bears in equally high esteem—in the shamanic tradition they would be her spirit animals. Henri had never seen an otter, but was fairly sure they did not deserve equal status with bears.

On the first morning, Lara jumped out of bed at dawn and rushed to the window. There was a pair of otters right out in front! Side by side in the soft pink light of sunrise, their feet and heads poking out of the calm water of the bay, they munched on their breakfast—perhaps a crab—the sound traveling clearly through the morning quiet.

Lara and Henri were both pleased to see them: to her, it was a sign that she was in the right place; to him, it was a relief to see that otters looked pretty much like wet seafaring bears. And as far as he was concerned, they were welcome to eat the crab; he preferred food he did not have to dive for! He was also glad to see Lara so delighted. The only drawback to that wonderful first sighting was that every morning after that, Lara jostled Henri out of bed for mandatory "Otter Watch" much earlier than he liked— earlier than even the otters themselves liked, apparently, as none turned up for the next six days in a row.

Fortunately, Henri was able to catch up on uninterrupted sleep, napping in the room while Lara attended her Tai Ji sessions. She came back to the room often—between sessions or before dinner—because the company of all the other participants seemed overwhelming at times. This surprised Henri. After all, she was a person too, wasn't she? And she liked other people?

"I came here for the Tai Ji, and the beauty of the place," she said. "I don't necessarily want to spend time with every other person who also decided to come." She sat down on the bed with a sigh. "I don't want to be unfriendly, but it's been a long time since I had to be polite and interested in strangers. It feels like a lot of work." If she attended any more out-of-town seminars, she decided, it would be with someone she'd like to have meals with.

Henri offered to be her dinner companion, if that would help, but Lara shook her head. "I think you'd draw *more* attention to my table," she laughed. "Prompting more conversations I don't really feel like having!"

At last, after a final happy sighting of the otters at dawn, the seminar was over. Later that day, Lucie welcomed Lara and Henri home with much tail wagging, and everyone was glad to be through with traveling for a while. Home is where the honey pot is, observed Henri, and where you like the person you share it with.

"I couldn't agree more," said Lara.

*

Henri was burrowed down under the covers on a November Monday morning. He woke up later and later these days, bearishly attuned to sunrise, and always in a peaceful, languid frame of mind. Perhaps this was hibernation California-style, he thought.

Lara, on the other hand, felt a tension rising within her by the day. For her, it felt like the respite was over. She had had her two short breaks, and now the burdens of her daily responsibilities—especially those concerning the failing health of her parents—were firmly back on her shoulders.

Taking them both to the doctor one day, she discovered that her dad had osteoporosis and needed to add a medication and calcium to his regimen, while her mom failed the memory test miserably, thinking it was May of 1973. Meanwhile, the eye drops her mom needed for glaucoma were not getting used, and the caretaker, Linda, couldn't always get them applied. Lara's dad was coughing worse than ever with his dysphagia—weak throat muscles. He needed an appointment with a speech therapist to learn exercises to reduce his risk of choking. By the time Lara got home, she was overwhelmed by all the appointments she needed to make. She had a bleak glimpse of a future in which she did nothing but drive around to doctors and specialists, and leaving her with no time to paint.

She slumped into a chair and looked at Henri. "How far should I be going with all this? How do I make decisions about their care when nothing is certain about the outcome?" She already knew what Pierre would have said: "Do only what must be done, and save your own time and life." But Lara worried too much for that. She was quick to feel selfish and guilty. She picked up the bear and held him tight—tighter than she had in months. He could feel the tension in her muscles, and recognized the familiar mixture of fear and sadness that she used to have so often.

"If Mom doesn't take her glaucoma drops she'll go blind," she said, "and if she's blind, her life will be even worse than it is now, for her and for me, and for the caretaker, too. I can't not respond."

He was a small bear, and still quite young, but Henri had learned a lot over his brief time with Lara, and he felt the importance of this moment. Lara was in danger of slipping back into the dark tunnel she'd been in when he first arrived. It was time to remind her of things that, in her anxiety and exhaustion, she was forgetting. So he made himself as soft as he could against the tightness in her hug, and he whispered to her to breathe…breathe…slowly, deeply. Then, as she did that, he began very quietly to remind her of all the rules by which she had survived Pierre's loss and rediscovered her own inner, creative strength.

Be present in the moment…right here, and right now, all is well; pay attention to that… *get your feet on the ground*…get up and do the things that need to be done; don't stew about it beforehand…*take lots of naps*…look after your body, and don't exhaust yourself: take help when it's offered, and have a massage...*get outside into nature*...go out for a sail this weekend; let the wind and the exercise clear your head of your worries...*create something*...keep one day this week to work on that new painting of Morro Bay, with that gorgeous light coming through the eucalyptus grove...and of course...*have some honey*...it will give you the strength to figure all this out.

Lara sat with her eyes closed, breathing and listening, until Henri felt the tension ease out of her body. Finally she opened her eyes and said, "I was wondering when you'd get around to mentioning honey." Then she kissed him on the nose.

They went into the kitchen and put the kettle on. Henri helped her think about and plan the week ahead; her parents would be cared for, and Friday would be a painting day, and Saturday she could get out and sail. The future suddenly seemed less bleak.

*

After the first week of November when Thanksgiving was around the corner, Lara pulled into the drive-through bank to deposit some checks in her parents' account. As she wrote out the deposit slips, tears started to trickle down her face.

Why here, and why now? she wondered. The obvious answer, of course, was that it was Pierre's birthday, which meant it was very nearly the anniversary of his death. But she had thought about that already, thought about *him*, as soon as she woke up that morning. So why was she blubbering then, in the car, while carrying out such a mundane task? Maybe because it was a neutral, anonymous place, she thought. But it felt like more than that, more as if time had folded back on itself, so that she suddenly felt again the enormous sense of loss that had overwhelmed her one year ago, the sheer shock of Pierre's no longer being around.

By the time the plastic capsule whooshed back through the tube from the teller, Lara's tears were falling freely. No Kleenex in the car. As she pulled away from the bank, she inadvertently flipped on the windshield wipers, but they did not dry her eyes.

When she got home, Henri was still at the breakfast table getting the last droplet of honey out of a special pot that he picked out in honor of Pierre's birthday. At breakfast he had given Lara the first taste. She had seemed cheerful, but now he saw her tear-stained face and knew she must have been crying in the car. Henri hoped that Lara did not feel she had to go off by herself to cry.

Lara looked at him. "I need to remember to keep some Kleenex in the car," she said. Henri replied that, in his opinion, tissues made a very poor substitute for a furry shoulder to cry on, and perhaps on difficult days like this, he should ride along in the car with her.

She nodded, thoughtfully. "You've put up with so much from me...are you sure you don't mind getting damp as well?" Henri looked slightly indignant at this, and pointed out that it was all part of his job. Also, his stuffing was highly absorbent and quick-drying.

"All right, then, I'll take you up on that," said Lara. "Well, I'm feeling wiped out. Are you ready for a nap?"

Henri reminded her that he was always ready for a nap, so they curled up together on the couch. But instead of falling asleep, Lara began at last to tell Henri the story she had never told him, of the sad day that Pierre, the big bear who was the love of her life, had left her.

"It started on the evening of his birthday," she said. "Well, no, actually, it started many months before that, when we learned that he had an aneurysm. The doctor told us he could die suddenly, at any moment. For weeks and weeks we all felt afraid, but Pierre carried on with life as usual, and he seemed well. After a while the fear sort of faded into the background.

"For his birthday, friends came over for dinner. I remember we had Champagne and gifts in front of the fire. Julie gave Pierre a framed photograph that she had taken of a rainbow. It was all so lovely. Then, during dinner, Pierre left the table. He was gone so long that I went to look for him and found him lying down. He said he felt unwell, but we should carry on with dinner. Later, Julie went to talk to him, and he was worse, in great pain. We called an ambulance."

Lara was quiet, then, for such a long time that Henri wondered if she had fallen asleep, but at last she continued: "They had told us with an aneurysm like that, death could be very quick. Three minutes, for some people...a few days at most. For Pierre, it was fifteen hours from when he got to the hospital to when he died. Not so long really, but still...it felt like the longest night of my life."

After that, Lara did not say any more; perhaps she slept, and maybe she cried a little, Henri was not sure. He just waited patiently, tucked in beside her, for this wave of grief to wash on through.

*

It was December, and the days had grown short. In the half light of one early morning, Lara found herself thinking about the goals that she had set for herself at the year's beginning. These had included: grieving fully, pushing her painting forward, being a good daughter to her parents, and listening more to her own daughter, Julie—trying to see her now twenty-two-year-old as someone separate from herself.

She felt that she had made progress in the first two: she loved painting in her new garage studio, and in recent weeks (with Henri's help) she had acknowledged and cared for that part of herself that was still so wounded by Pierre's loss. In her relationship with Julie, Lara felt herself growing into the new role of mother to an adult child, and she trusted that the holiday season would give the two of them some opportunity for meaningful time together.

But this morning was her mother's birthday, so Lara's mind was on her role as daughter. She had not expected to feel so excited about the event—even happy occasions with her mother could be emotionally wearing—but this birthday felt like a major milestone. It was the first time any female in her family had reached the age of ninety-one, and Lara knew that, as a care-giver, she had played a part in helping her fragile hundred-pound mother live to see this day.

She felt a surge of love and enthusiasm, and jumped decisively out of bed, jostling Henri from a happy dream. He was about to win a honey lottery, he told her crossly, and now it was all gone.

"Sorry, Henri, but it's Mom's birthday," said Lara, bustling into the kitchen, "and I actually feel like loving her, gnarly and difficult as she sometimes is."

On the kitchen table everything stood ready for her to take over to her parents' house: a little Christmas tree, which she had made out of a rosemary plant and decorated with miniature ornaments and tiny lights; a pair of new pink flannel pajamas; chocolate-covered cookies; jars of pickled red beets and red cabbage with apple—treats to remind Mom of her own mom, who prepared those German dishes so well.

At a quarter to nine, Lara telephoned her mother. When the familiar little squeaky voice answered, Lara sang Happy Birthday, stretching out the "to you" and "Mom" parts, to fill them with extra love. Lara felt as if she had been sprinkled with magic fairy dust: the normal rancor she felt around her mother was gone. Mom giggled a little at the other end of the phone, and announced they had just sat down for breakfast.

"Well, I'll let you go, then, so you can have a nice birthday breakfast," said Lara. "But I'll be over soon, with your gifts."

As she carried the boxes and the little tree out to her car, Henri pointed out that it was still early to be paying a birthday visit. He himself did not like to be interrupted during breakfast.

"But this way," explained Lara, "she'll feel loved all day with her gifts, and I'll still be able to take care of my normal Wednesday activities." She was eager to share this joyful occasion with her mother, to nurture the surge of love she had felt towards her this morning.

But as soon as she arrived at the house, Lara thought that Henri might be right. Her parents were still having breakfast—she often forgot how slowly things got done at this point in their lives. Though Lara urged them to stay where they were and enjoy their meal, Mom immediately got up from the table, as if she ought to be doing something about the fuss being made over her. She moved around the room restlessly, speaking in the angry, frustrated voice Lara knew so well, complaining that her clothes had no pockets, and she had nowhere to put her Kleenex.

Lara gave her a long birthday hug, wrapping the little birdlike body tight in her arms. Her mom did not relax into it, but stayed tense, as if the hug might be dangerous or make her fall down. However, she did make a little noise like it was good. Then she wanted to open her presents right away.

"Why don't you finish your coffee first? It's getting cold," said Lara. But Mom was already tearing the wrapping off a small box.

"Is there any chocolate?" she asked eagerly, avid as a child for her candy, and then was disappointed when it turned out to be chocolate-covered cookies rather than a box of chocolates.

Lara realized that she should leave. Henri was definitely right; Mom mainly wanted to be left alone and go at her own pace, with not even the demand of receiving gifts that required a response. Being celebrated felt awkward to her; she could not enjoy it, and therefore could not say thank you. If Lara's goal was to be a good daughter to her mom, she needed to accept that about her.

"I'll be going now," said Lara, "but Julie and I will see you on Saturday, for a birthday meal and cake." She gave her mom a quick hug. "Go on and finish your breakfast now; I'm sorry I interrupted you."

On the drive home, she pictured her mom eating a chocolate-covered cookie with her cold coffee, and never finishing her cereal. She sighed and shook her head, then remembered something that the Hospice counselor had said to her: "Your mother is never going to be any different than she always was; if anything, her characteristics will become exacerbated."

At home, Lara swept Henri up for a good hug, and told him how the visit had gone. He heard the disappointment in her voice and had the good grace not to say "I told you so."

"It feels as if I am always trying to figure out how to love her in a way she can accept," said Lara.

That part was easy for bears, Henri told her. They just share their favorite food.

"I know: the way to a bear's heart is through his honey-pot," said Lara. "But that's not necessarily true for everyone. I'm not sure it's true for me."

But the more she thought about it, the more Lara saw that in fact it was somewhat true for her. She could think of several good friendships that were maintained solely on the basis of mutual enjoyment of good food. And it would not be a chore to make her mother's favorite dinner; that would give Lara pleasure, as well.

She busied herself with the planning and details, driving here and there to get just the right ingredients to create a real *choucroute*, as Pierre would have called the sauerkraut and sausage dish her mother relished. And for dessert, to go with the all-important double chocolate cake, Lara also took the trouble to whip up fresh cream with a touch of vanilla extract and a little sugar. She smiled in anticipation: whipped cream was the one thing that could reliably make her mother sparkle with happiness.

Sure enough, the bowl of cream stayed next to her mother throughout dessert, and Lara watched with pleasure and amusement as a dollop of cream was added to *each bite* of cake. If that were not enough indication that the dinner was a success, the phone call from her mother the next morning removed all doubt.

"She called, Henri! To say thank you!" said Lara in surprised delight. "You were right. Cooking is definitely the most effective love language, as far as my mother and I are concerned."

Henri pretended to be surprised as well, although privately he felt a quiet satisfaction that things had turned out exactly as he had predicted.

*

About a week after the birthday dinner, Julie phoned Lara in great excitement: "Hey, Mom, you won't believe this! I got free tickets to the taping of the *Ellen* Show for December 13. You wanna go with me?"

Lara, surprised by the invitation—she had never even seen the show on TV —was even more surprised to hear herself answer "Yes!" Normally, the idea of going to Los Angeles, finding the NBC Studios in Burbank, standing in line for six hours, and driving home again, would have seemed like a nightmare.

Her decision to go had nothing to do with Ellen Degeneres, though she had the impression that Ellen was a funny, gutsy woman. It had everything to do with the goal she had set for herself at the year's beginning: to be more available to her daughter, and to get to know the young adult she was becoming.

Julie was often frustrated with her mom. Lara was not always a good listener, and would occasionally forget the things Julie told her: dates and times of finals, planned visits from friends, even secrets. Julie saw this as evidence of her mother's lack of interest in the details of her life; Lara knew she loved her daughter, but saw that she was too full of her own ideas about Julie's life, and not always truly open to the real Julie.

Pierre's death had affected both mother and daughter terribly, but they had suffered differently. Julie had lost one of the two main pillars of strength in her life. Her initial fear, as they left the hospital after keeping vigil through Pierre's last night, was that she literally *could not live* without her papa. Lara, by contrast, knew she would go on living; her only question was how she would adapt to that new life.

But adapt she had, over the course of this year. Now she felt more able to give Julie the attention she deserved, and this was the perfect occasion to start. Julie's delight at getting tickets to the show was a pleasure to behold, and Lara felt honored to have been invited to share in the event.

Henri was skeptical. He had watched the Ellen show once, snuggled up with Julie one afternoon, and he mainly remembered the people in the audience dancing around and screaming a lot. Also, there were lots of commercials for things nobody needs, and *not one* for honey! Lara was prepared to stand in line all day for that?

"You're right. It really isn't my sort of thing," said Lara. "But it is Julie's sort of thing, and that's why I'm so pleased she's invited me! I may not get many more chances to share the exciting events in her life. And who knows? It might be interesting to see how they make TV shows."

Henri remained unconvinced, and suggested it would be much nicer to have a quiet day in the studio, painting.

Lara looked out of the window thoughtfully, her eyes resting on Lucie, who was lying in a patch of sunshine. Then she said, "I learned a long time ago, when I moved alone to France to paint, that painting is not my whole existence. It does not fill me up like a good human relationship. This excursion to LA could be a total fiasco, or it could be a lark, but either way, I'd be with someone who means the world to me. I'm going."

Henri did not raise any further objections. Underneath his disapproval he was quite pleased that Lara had chosen to do something adventurous with her daughter.

Julie and Lara drove down to LA the day before the show, having made plans to stay in the city with friends. Barry and Martha had been with them the night Pierre died, sharing the last Champagne Pierre ever drank, together by the fire before his birthday dinner. Since then, whenever the four of them were together, they were reminded of this poignant bond. Although they didn't speak of it, the undercurrent was there, and the first toast was always to Pierre.

The drive down the Pacific Coast Highway was a pleasure, with the pink late afternoon light on the ocean, waves frothing onto shore, and pelicans diving after fish. Julie and Lara exclaimed at the beauty of the coast they were lucky enough to call home, all the while discussing Julie's plan to move to Europe for a couple of years, and Lara's desire to go over there, too. Two women, equally greedy for life, hopping from one delicious topic to another.

Within minutes of their arrival at Barry and Martha's house, the Champagne was opened and Pierre was remembered just as he would have wished: with love and laughter. Later, after a delicious Italian meal, when Julie and Lara started getting to settle into the guest room for the night, Lara realized she had not brought Henri along on this trip.

For the first time in eleven months she would be climbing into bed without his furry, comforting presence. She wondered why she had left him behind. Was it because he hadn't liked the idea of the trip in the first place? Or was it because she did not need him as much as she used to? Being without him felt strange, but she did not feel bereft. Shifts were taking place.

The next morning it was clear to Lara that shifts were happening in Julie, as well: she was taking on more responsibility and acting on her intentions. She had researched the Internet for a map of exactly how to get to NBC in Burbank, printed it out, verified the efficiency of it with Barry, gotten up at eight a.m.—an unheard-of hour for her—and was cheerfully ready to leave by nine. Lara had never seen her daughter so full of purpose and energy.

Before getting into the car, Julie made a complete check of her Mom's appearance, as if Lara were going for an audience with the Pope. Lara passed the test and got into the passenger's seat, fully aware of how their roles were changing. Then they set out into the spaghetti bowl of LA's freeways to find Burbank and the NBC studio. Julie saw that the line had already formed and screeched to a halt, letting Lara out to secure a spot, while she went on a parking quest.

There were about eighty people installed on folding chairs with bags and blankets, like people waiting for a parade. Lara had a quick flashback to Henri's gloomy predictions about the day. He was right: she was cold, the curb was hard to sit on, and the nearest bathroom was quite a trot away.

Just as Lara was having second thoughts, Julie came striding up the sidewalk, victorious after finding a perfect parking place right around the corner. She smiled broadly, her eyes filled with glee at being mere hours away from "meeting" Ellen in person. As soon as she saw Julie's face and felt her joyful hug, Lara adjusted her perspective and felt her own enthusiasm return.

They settled in with a towel to cushion their seat on the curb. About an hour into their wait, a silver Porsche approached and slowed. The car's window slid open and there was Ellen, yelling "Hi, everybody!" The cheery greeting removed Lara's worry that the show might be cancelled for some reason, and they would have come all this way for nothing. The star had shown up for work. There would indeed be a show.

Time crept on. The sun started to warm them up nicely. Lara and Julie nibbled from the bag of mandarins from Lara's garden and drank water.

In the early afternoon, things started to happen: everyone received a number and went through a security check. Just like at an airport, each person was frisked with a wand and handbags were searched: no sharp objects—not even knitting needles—allowed. Then they were herded towards a long line of benches and told to sit. Again. Another long wait, but this time they could watch TV monitors playing Ellen's show from the day before. Then the production staff announced a delay, as the special musical guest was still doing his sound check. Julie groaned: "I think I've hit my limit for how long I'll wait for something, even something this good." Lara thought to herself: *Amen.*

Finally—after instructions about when to scream and dance and when not to—it was time to move in to the studio. Lara and Julie were directed to separate seats. Julie got to be front row center and was ecstatic; Lara was farther up in the next section over, but they could see each other.

The music started blaring, and the crowd started dancing. Ellen liked for people to dance on her show—she herself joined in, coming up into the audience to dance. Lara liked the sense of joy and frolic that radiated from her, balancing her dry, sarcastic wit.

The special guest was Stevie Wonder, whose manner was as warm as his voice, slow and soothing. Blind since early childhood, he spoke of how he imagined color in his music. Then, after he performed one of his songs, a little bell sounded, and a man in a huge gingerbread-man-cookie costume danced in from the wings. The audience erupted into deafening applause. It turned out that this was one of "Twelve Days of Christmas," and Ellen was about to reveal a series of gifts to be given to every person in the audience. With her characteristic playfulness, she pulled lids off one box after another, announcing gifts worth hundreds of dollars. Lara's jaw dropped with amazement.

Somehow this whole experience was turning into Christmas Eve. Even Lara was totally immersed in the wonder of it all. Henri wouldn't believe it if he could see her now. She was dancing, shouting, smiling, and laughing—in the last month of the most difficult year of her life. She felt grateful. Grateful and glad that she accepted Julie's invitation and took this chance, that had turned into an exceptional experience they could share.

The hour flew by. Soon they were walking out into the night and packing the little blue Prius full to the brim with their gifts. Their spirits were high, even though they were exhausted from the long wait, and from the high energy of the show itself. They chattered back and forth, reliving the details of their day, and in the excitement managed to get lost in the labyrinth of LA's freeways. When they finally found the road to take them home, Lara started to relax. Julie was a good driver, and Lara could enjoy being the passenger, with no responsibility. As she looked out of her window at the lights streaming past in the night, Lara thought back to her goals for the year, and felt that this one—to connect more intentionally with Julie—had been achieved in a way she could never have anticipated, amid a flurry of Hollywood sparkle. Arriving home, they carried Lara's share of the gifts into the house, while Lucie ran back and forth in contagious joy and excitement. Then Lara thanked Julie for the great day, and for doing all the driving. They hugged and kissed goodnight by the Christmas tree, breathing in the smell of the Douglas Fir.

When Julie had gone, Lara went into the kitchen. Henri was sitting there, near the toaster. Lara began to tell him all about the show, and unpacked some of her shiny new pots and pans, for him to see. He pretended to be unimpressed, and said that a lifetime's supply of honey would have been a much more useful gift

Lara smiled and picked him up. "*That's* what was missing from my day! I haven't heard the word honey even once!" Then she gave him a long hug, which felt good to both of them.

As they headed for bed, Henri noticed a definite lilt in Lara's step. She chatted cheerfully before sleep, and when she closed her eyes and began to breathe slowly and deeply, Henri found that he was no longer in an airtight lock of a hug. Lara held him gently. Something had changed.

He had thought she would hate this trip to LA, but maybe he had been thinking of the Lara he had first met, the fearful person who could not get out of bed in the morning. He knew that this new lightness of spirit he sensed in her had nothing to do with the TV show, or the shiny new gifts. It seemed more as if she had remembered that the world still held good things for her, and that it could be fun to go out and find them. Maybe Lara was coming back to her old self, the capable person she was before Pierre's passing. His Lara was getting stronger, more adventurous.

Henri stared at the ceiling, thinking back through the year. So much had happened, so much had changed, and all of it had brought them to that moment when Lara left him at home alone. That had seemed strange, being by himself in the empty bed, but he had not felt sad, only uncertain of how she might be doing, out there in the world on her own. Now, the thought of her flourishing again, even without him, filled him with joy—and a little warm glow of satisfaction, at having completed the task that Julie had given him. He and Lara would always be fast friends, he knew, and he would be here in case she lost ground, but maybe now he could let go of his vigilant role a little bit.

With that in mind, Henri drifted off to sleep planning his own goals for the coming year. It was not a long list. He would take more naps, spend more time in the garden watching the bees, and eat more—*lots* more—delicious, golden honey.

This was a year of changes, a year in which Lara learned how to move forward and open up to life's possibilities again, thanks to words and acts of wisdom from many sources. Henri's advice was as simple and comforting as his presence: take plenty of naps, and eat plenty of honey. Here are some of the other wise words that helped, and which might help you, or someone you care about, facing a similar loss.

❖ Hit the ground in the morning: straight out of bed, and get going.

❖ Get outside and breathe in the immensity of nature.

❖ Don't read bad news with your morning toast.

❖ Stay in the present moment; life is almost always good in the NOW.

❖ Go and do something that you like (even if it's buying compost!).

❖ Expect to feel strange and disoriented for a long time.

❖ Focus on the small, reliable things.

❖ Shift your focus from mind to body, and start moving.

❖ Create something. Don't think too hard: go straight from your heart to the canvas.

❖ Act the way you want to feel.

❖ Tackle daunting tasks with an enthusiastic friend, if possible, and soon.

❖ Put a regular massage on your schedule, and in your budget; it's not an indulgence.

❖ Master a new skill: facing one challenge makes the next one less frightening.

❖ Write to the person you have lost. Get the words out of your head and onto the page.

❖ Take help when it is offered.

❖ Remember that your life may have changed, but you are still you, and the world still holds joys and opportunities that will reveal themselves little by little.

Tana Sommer-Belin is a native Californian who has spent much of her adult life in Europe, primarily in France, where she met her husband. After his death in 2003, Tana began to write the story held in this book. Though fictionalized, it remains a potent and deeply true account of one woman's first year of loss.

A lifelong artist working mainly in oil and watercolor, Tana has practiced etching, photography, drawing and ceramics. She is also a published poet. Her current artistic production and biography may be seen on her web site: www.tanasommer.com.

Tana Sommer-Belin now divides her year between California and the Perche region of France. She may occasionally be glimpsed in the company of a well-worn stuffed bear.

www.ingramcontent.com/pod-product-compliance
Lightning Source LLC
Chambersburg PA
CBHW020518030426
42337CB00011B/446